3 SONATAS

for Flute, Harpsichord & Viola da Gamba

mm

3340

MUSIC MINUS ONE
Flute or Alto Recorder

Music Minus One

Three Sonatas For Flute, Harpischord & Viola da Gamba

PRINTED IN CANADA

G. P. TELEMANN
TRIO IN F MAJOR

Editing Suggestions
by Jean Antrim

6 taps precede music.

Vivace

4

5

Introduction to Ornamentation

Contemporary knowledge of style and practice in the 17th and 18th centuries is gained by studying a number of meticulously prepared treatises in the form of "tutors" or "methods" by the great teachers of the period. Certainly among the most valuable of these documents stands the "Essay of a Method for Playing the Transverse Flute" written by Johann Joachim Quantz in 1752. Having conscientiously lived through the tradition of the "High Baroque", Quantz was well equipped to preserve his first hand experiences and information for the edification of his contemporaries. The Essay, a giant of baroque musical literature, not only provides an excellent tutor for achieving technical mastery on the flute, but covers inexhaustible details of 18th century performance practice and taste.

Never preoccupied with the ideal of music for posterity, the baroque musician was primarily concerned with providing works for specific needs; music to be performed at the time, using whatever resources available to the occasion. Musical compositions were judged by their intrinsic qualities, the medium of performance considered quite secondary; therefore, alterations to suit the occasional need — instrumental substitutions, key transposition, abbreviations and extensions offered no serious concern to either performer or composer.

The overabundance of editorial markings dealing with dynamics, articulation and tempo to which the modern player is fettered were relatively foreign to the baroque manuscript, thereby inviting the tasteful and inventive performer to participate more intimately in the composer's efforts. In many instances scores were looked upon as mere suggestions or skeletons on which the musical essence could be enhanced and elaborated upon according to a traditional vocabulary of performance customs. The art of extempore, or spontaneous ornamentation on given notes or themes was as ordinary and commonplace as it was highly sophisticated, marking the baroque era as one of the most personal and eloquent periods of musical creativity.

Baroque ornaments may be explained in two classes: those categorized according to a prevalent system of signs, and those freely improvised. Fortunately for the historically aware performer, detailed ornamentation tables have been efficiently prepared by several old masters and one needs only to study the signs and their explication to arrive at the proper execution. In many cases, discrepancies of actual signs and terms appeared according to time and locale, but the basic method of delivery remained uniform. Several different tables of the most frequently used signed embellishments have been included to illustrate the minor points of discrepancy. Of these ornaments, the *trill* (basically an ornamented appoggiatura) is the most common and characteristic of the baroque, inspiring a wealth of written explanations as to its significance and appropriate handling.

— Shakes —

" Shakes add great lustre to one's playing, and, like appoggiaturas, are quite indispensable. If an instrumentalist or singer were to possess all the skill required by good taste in performance, and yet could not strike good shakes, his total art would be incomplete. While nature stands one person in good stead in this respect, another must learn the shake through much application. Some players succeed with all their fingers, some with only a few, and for still others the shake remains throughout life a stumbling-block presumably more dependent upon the constitution of the man's tendons than upon his will. With industry, however, many improvements can be made, if the player does not expect the shake to come by itself, and if, while his fingers are still growing, he takes the requisite pains to perfect it.

All shakes do not have to be struck with the same speed; in this matter you must be governed by the place in which you are playing, as well as by the piece to be performed. If playing in a large place which reverberates strongly, a somewhat slower shake will be more effective than a quicker one; for too rapid an alternation of notes is confused through the reverberation, and this makes the shake indistinct. In a small or tapestried room, on the other hand, where the listeners are close by, a quicker shake will be better than a slower one. In addition, you must be able to distinguish the character of each piece you play, so that you do not confuse those of one sort with those of another, as many do. In melancholy pieces the shake must be struck more slowly, in gay ones, more quickly.

Slowness or quickness, however, must not be excessive. The very slow shake is customary only in French singing, and is of as little use as the very quick, trembling one, which the French call *chevroté* (bleating). You must not be misled even if some of the greatest and most celebrated singers execute the shake chiefly in the latter fashion. Although many, from ignor-

ance, indeed consider this bleating shake a special merit, they do not know that a moderately quick and even shake is much more difficult to learn than the very fast trembling one, and that the latter must therefore be considered a defect.

The *shake in thirds* in which the third, instead of the adjacent second, is struck above the principal note, although customary of old, and still the mode nowadays among some Italian violinists and oboists, must not be used either in singing or playing (except, perhaps, upon the bagpipe). Each shake must take up no more than the interval of a whole tone or a semitone, as is required by the key, and by the note upon which the shake originates.

If the shake is to be genuinely beautiful, it must be played evenly, or at a uniform and moderate speed. Upon instruments, therefore, the fingers must never be raised higher at one stroke than at another. "

All ornaments are played *on the beat,* the reason being twofold: to avoid rhythmic and melodic distortion, and to provide the spice of dissonance to a fundamentally consonant harmonic style. Quantz elucidates the 18th century thought on dissonance:

— Dissonance —

"To excite the different passions, the dissonances must be struck more strongly than the consonances. Consonances make the spirit peaceful and tranquil; dissonances, on the other hand, disturb it. Just as an uninterrupted pleasure of whatever kind it might be, would weaken and exhaust our capacities for remaining sensitive to it until the pleasure finally ceased, so a long series of pure consonances would eventually cause the ear distaste and displeasure, if they were not mingled now and then with disagreeable sounds such as those produced by dissonances. The more then that a dissonance is distinguished and set off from other notes in playing, the more it affects the ear. But the more displeasing the disturbance of our pleasure, the more agreeable the ensuing pleasure seems to us. Then the harsher the dissonance, the more pleasing is its resolution. Without this mixture of agreeable and disagreeable sounds, music would no longer be able now to arouse the different passions instantly, now to still them again."

Regarding the addition of free improvised ornaments, Quantz provides ample suggestions of which a few are given here.

The player may experiment with these examples, in the appropriate places or invent his own as inspired from the style and character of each composition. In the use of both signed and improvised ornamentation, however, the performer is cautioned to use discretion as a guide and heed the following advice from Quantz:

— Extempore —

"Variations must be undertaken only after the plain air has already been heard; otherwise the listener cannot know if the variations are actually present. A well written melody which is already sufficiently pleasing in itself, must never be varied, unless you believe it can be improved. If you wish to vary something, you must always do it in such fashion that the addition is still more agreeable in the singing phrases, and still more brilliant in the passage work, than they stand as written. Not a little insight and experience are required for this. Without an understanding of composition, success is impossible. Those who lack the skill will always do better to prefer the invention of the composer to their own fancies. A long series of quick notes does not always suffice. They may, indeed, excite admiration, but they do not touch the heart as easily as plain notes, and this after all is the true object of music, and the most difficult one. Here also a great abuse has crept in. Therefore my advice is not to give yourself over too much to variations, but rather to apply yourself to playing a plain air nobly, truly, and clearly.

In general you must always see to it in the variations that the principal notes, on which variations are made, are not obscured. If variations are introduced on crochets usually the first note of the variations must be the same as the plain note; and you proceed in the same fashion with all the other values, whether they are greater or less than a crochet. To be sure, another note may be chosen from the harmony of the bass, but the principal note must then be heard immediately after it."

Source: In Playing The Flute
J. J. Quantz

Source: In Playing The Flute J. J. Quantz

Of Extempore Variations on Simple Intervals

G.F. HANDEL
SONATA NO.3 IN C MAJOR

8 taps precede music.
Larghetto

Editing Suggestions
by Jean Antrim

* Ornamentation Optional

6 *taps precede music.* Allegro

9

Larghetto*

* Ornamentation optional

10

4 taps precede music.

A tempo di Gavotti

Allegro   6 taps precede music.

G. P. TELEMANN
TRIO SONATA IN Bb MAJOR

Editing Suggestions
by Jean Antrim

* Cadenza optional

MMO CD 3340

12

Siciliana   **6** taps precede music.

* Ornamentation optional

14

4 taps precede music.

MMO Compact Disc Catalog

BROADWAY

LES MISERABLES/PHANTOM OF THE OPERA	MMO CD 1016
HITS OF ANDREW LLOYD WEBBER	MMO CD 1054
GUYS AND DOLLS	MMO CD 1067
WEST SIDE STORY 2 CD Set	MMO CD 1100
CABARET 2 CD Set	MMO CD 1110
BROADWAY HEROES AND HEROINES	MMO CD 1121
CAMELOT	MMO CD 1173
BEST OF ANDREW LLOYD WEBBER	MMO CD 1130
THE SOUND OF BROADWAY	MMO CD 1133
BROADWAY MELODIES	MMO CD 1134
BARBRA'S BROADWAY	MMO CD 1144
JEKYLL & HYDE	MMO CD 1151
SHOWBOAT	MMO CD 1160
MY FAIR LADY 2 CD Set	MMO CD 1174
OKLAHOMA!	MMO CD 1175
THE SOUND OF MUSIC 2 CD Set	MMO CD 1176
SOUTH PACIFIC	MMO CD 1177
THE KING AND I	MMO CD 1178
FIDDLER ON THE ROOF 2 CD Set	MMO CD 1179
CAROUSEL	MMO CD 1180
PORGY AND BESS	MMO CD 1181
THE MUSIC MAN	MMO CD 1183
ANNIE GET YOUR GUN 2 CD Set	MMO CD 1186
HELLO DOLLY! 2 CD Set	MMO CD 1187
OLIVER 2 CD Set	MMO CD 1189
SUNSET BOULEVARD	MMO CD 1193
GREASE	MMO CD 1196
SMOKEY JOE'S CAFE	MMO CD 1197
MISS SAIGON	MMO CD 1226

CLARINET

MOZART CONCERTO, IN A	MMO CD 3201
WEBER CONCERTO NO. 1 in Fm. STAMITZ CONC. No. 3 IN Bb	MMO CD 3202
SPOHR CONCERTO NO. 1 in C MINOR OP. 26	MMO CD 3203
WEBER CONCERTO OP. 26, BEETHOVEN TRIO OP. 11	MMO CD 3204
FIRST CHAIR CLARINET SOLOS	MMO CD 3205
THE ART OF THE SOLO CLARINET:	MMO CD 3206
MOZART QUINTET IN A, K.581	MMO CD 3207
BRAHMS SONATAS OP. 120 NO. 1 & 2	MMO CD 3208
WEBER GRAND DUO CONCERTANT WAGNER ADAGIO	MMO CD 3209
SCHUMANN FANTASY OP. 73, 3 ROMANCES OP. 94	MMO CD 3210
EASY CLARINET SOLOS Volume 1 - STUDENT LEVEL	MMO CD 3211
EASY CLARINET SOLOS Volume 2 - STUDENT LEVEL	MMO CD 3212
EASY JAZZ DUETS - STUDENT LEVEL	MMO CD 3213
BEGINNING CONTEST SOLOS - Jerome Bunke, Clinician	MMO CD 3221
BEGINNING CONTEST SOLOS - Harold Wright	MMO CD 3222
INTERMEDIATE CONTEST SOLOS - Stanley Drucker	MMO CD 3223
INTERMEDIATE CONTEST SOLOS - Jerome Bunke, Clinician	MMO CD 3224
ADVANCED CONTEST SOLOS - Stanley Drucker	MMO CD 3225
ADVANCED CONTEST SOLOS - Harold Wright	MMO CD 3226
INTERMEDIATE CONTEST SOLOS - Stanley Drucker	MMO CD 3227
ADVANCED CONTEST SOLOS - Stanley Drucker	MMO CD 3228
ADVANCED CONTEST SOLOS - Harold Wright	MMO CD 3229
BRAHMS Clarinet Quintet in Am, Op. 115	MMO CD 3230
TEACHER'S PARTNER Basic Clarinet Studies	MMO CD 3231
JEWELS FOR WOODWIND QUINTET	MMO CD 3232
WOODWIND QUINTETS minus CLARINET	MMO CD 3233

PIANO

BEETHOVEN CONCERTO NO 1 IN C	MMO CD 3001
BEETHOVEN CONCERTO NO. 2 IN Bb	MMO CD 3002
BEETHOVEN CONCERTO NO. 3 IN C MINOR	MMO CD 3003
BEETHOVEN CONCERTO NO. 4 IN G	MMO CD 3004
BEETHOVEN CONCERTO NO. 5 IN Eb (2 CD SET)	MMO CD 3005
GRIEG CONCERTO IN A MINOR OP.16	MMO CD 3006
RACHMANINOFF CONCERTO NO. 2 IN C MINOR	MMO CD 3007
SCHUMANN CONCERTO IN A MINOR	MMO CD 3008
BRAHMS CONCERTO NO. 1 IN D MINOR (2 CD SET)	MMO CD 3009
CHOPIN CONCERTO NO. 1 IN E MINOR OP. 11	MMO CD 3010
MENDELSSOHN CONCERTO NO. 1 IN G MINOR	MMO CD 3011
MOZART CONCERTO NO. 9 IN Eb K.271	MMO CD 3012
MOZART CONCERTO NO. 12 IN A K.414	MMO CD 3013
MOZART CONCERTO NO. 20 IN D MINOR K.466	MMO CD 3014
MOZART CONCERTO NO. 23 IN A K.488	MMO CD 3015
MOZART CONCERTO NO. 24 IN C MINOR K.491	MMO CD 3016
MOZART CONCERTO NO. 26 IN D K.537, CORONATION	MMO CD 3017
MOZART CONCERTO NO. 17 IN G K.453	MMO CD 3018
LISZT CONCERTO NO. 1 IN Eb, WEBER OP. 79	MMO CD 3019
LISZT CONCERTO NO. 2 IN A, HUNGARIAN FANTASIA	MMO CD 3020
J.S. BACH CONCERTO IN F MINOR, J.C. BACH CON. IN Eb	MMO CD 3021
J.S. BACH CONCERTO IN D MINOR	MMO CD 3022
HAYDN CONCERTO IN D	MMO CD 3023
HEART OF THE PIANO CONCERTO	MMO CD 3024
THEMES FROM GREAT PIANO CONCERTI	MMO CD 3025
TSCHAIKOVSKY CONCERTO NO. 1 IN Bb MINOR	MMO CD 3026
ART OF POPULAR PIANO PLAYING, Vol. 1 STUDENT LEVEL	MMO CD 3033
ART OF POPULAR PIANO PLAYING, Vol. 2 STUDENT LEVEL 2 CD Set	MMO CD 3034
'POP' PIANO FOR STARTERS STUDENT LEVEL	MMO CD 3035
MOZART COMPLETE MUSIC FOR PIANO FOUR HANDS 2 CD Set	MMO CD 3036
DVORAK TRIO IN A MAJOR, OP. 90 "Dumky Trio"	MMO CD 3037
DVORAK QUINTET IN A MAJOR, OP. 81	MMO CD 3038
MENDELSSOHN TRIO IN D MAJOR, OP. 49	MMO CD 3039
MENDELSSOHN TRIO IN C MINOR, OP. 66	MMO CD 3040

PIANO - FOUR HANDS

RACHMANINOFF Six Scenes	4-5th year	MMO CD 3027
ARENSKY 6 Pieces, STRAVINSKY 3 Easy Dances	2-3rd year	MMO CD 3028
FAURE Dolly Suite	3-4th year	MMO CD 3029
DEBUSSY Petite Suite	3-4th year	MMO CD 3030

SCHUMANN Pictures from the East	4-5th year	MMO CD 3031
BEETHOVEN Three Marches	4-5th year	MMO CD 3032
MAYKAPAR First Steps, OP. 29	1-2nd year	MMO CD 3041
TSCHAIKOVSKY Fifty Russian Folk Songs	1-2nd year	MMO CD 3042

INSTRUCTIONAL METHODS

RUTGERS UNIVERSITY MUSIC DICTATION/EAR TRAINING COURSE (7 CD Set)	MMO CD 7001
EVOLUTION OF THE BLUES	MMO CD 7004
THE ART OF IMPROVISATION, VOL. 1	MMO CD 7005
THE ART OF IMPROVISATION, VOL. 2	MMO CD 7006
THE BLUES MINUS YOU Ed Xiques, Soloist	MMO CD 7007
TAKE A CHORUS minus Bb/Eb Instruments	MMO CD 7008

VIOLIN

BRUCH CONCERTO NO. 1 IN G MINOR OP.26	MMO CD 3100
MENDELSSOHN CONCERTO IN E MINOR	MMO CD 3101
TSCHAIKOVSKY CONCERTO IN D OP. 35	MMO CD 3102
BACH DOUBLE CONCERTO IN D MINOR	MMO CD 3103
BACH CONCERTO IN A MINOR, CONCERTO IN E	MMO CD 3104
BACH BRANDENBURG CONCERTI NOS. 4 & 5	MMO CD 3105
BACH BRANDENBURG CONCERTO NO. 2, TRIPLE CONCERTO	MMO CD 3106
BACH CONCERTO IN DM, (FROM CONCERTO FOR HARPSICHORD)	MMO CD 3107
BRAHMS CONCERTO IN D OP. 77	MMO CD 3108
CHAUSSON POEME, SCHUBERT RONDO	MMO CD 3109
LALO SYMPHONIE ESPAGNOLE	MMO CD 3110
MOZART CONCERTO IN D K.218, VIVALDI CON. AM OP.3 NO.6	MMO CD 3111
MOZART CONCERTO IN A K.219	MMO CD 3112
WIENIAWSKI CON. IN D. SARASATE ZIGEUNERWEISEN	MMO CD 3113
VIOTTI CONCERTO NO.22	MMO CD 3114
BEETHOVEN 2 ROMANCES, SONATA NO. 5 IN F "SPRING SONATA"	MMO CD 3115
SAINT-SAENS INTRODUCTION & RONDO.	
MOZART SERENADE K. 204, ADAGIO K.261	MMO CD 3116
BEETHOVEN CONCERTO IN D OP. 61(2 CD SET)	MMO CD 3117
THE CONCERTMASTER	MMO CD 3118
AIR ON A G STRING Favorite Encores with Orchestra Easy Medium	MMO CD 3119
CONCERT PIECES FOR THE SERIOUS VIOLINIST Easy Medium	MMO CD 3120
18TH CENTURY VIOLIN PIECES	MMO CD 3121
ORCHESTRAL FAVORITES - Volume 1 - Easy Level	MMO CD 3122
ORCHESTRAL FAVORITES - Volume 2 - Medium Level	MMO CD 3123
ORCHESTRAL FAVORITES - Volume 3 - Med to Difficult Level	MMO CD 3124
THE THREE B'S BACH/BEETHOVEN/BRAHMS	MMO CD 3125
VIVALDI Concerto in A Minor Op. 3 No. 6. in D Op. 3 No. 9.	
Double Concerto Op. 3 No. 8	MMO CD 3126
VIVALDI-THE FOUR SEASONS (2 CD Set)	MMO CD 3127
VIVALDI Concerto in Eb, Op. 8, No. 5. ALBINONI Concerto in A	MMO CD 3128
VIVALDI Concerto in E, Op. 3, No. 12. Concerto in C Op. 8, No. 6 "Il Piacere"	MMO CD 3129
SCHUBERT Three Sonatinas	MMO CD 3130
HAYDN String Quartet Op. 76 No. 1	MMO CD 3131
HAYDN String Quartet Op. 76 No. 2	MMO CD 3132
HAYDN String Quartet Op. 76 No. 3 "Emperor"	MMO CD 3133
HAYDN String Quartet Op. 76 No. 4 "Sunrise"	MMO CD 3134
HAYDN String Quartet Op. 76 No. 5	MMO CD 3135
HAYDN String Quartet Op. 76 No. 6	MMO CD 3136
BEAUTIFUL MUSIC FOR TWO VIOLINS 1st position, vol. 1	MMO CD 3137 ★
BEAUTIFUL MUSIC FOR TWO VIOLINS 2nd position, vol. 2	MMO CD 3138 ★
BEAUTIFUL MUSIC FOR TWO VIOLINS 3rd position, vol. 3	MMO CD 3139 ★
BEAUTIFUL MUSIC FOR TWO VIOLINS 1st, 2nd, 3rd position, vol. 4	MMO CD 3140 ★
BARTOK: 44 DUETS	MMO CD 3141
TEACHER'S PARTNER Basic Violin Studies 1st year	MMO CD 3142
DVORAK STRING TRIO "Terzetto", OP. 74 2 violins/viola	MMO CD 3143

★Lovely folk tunes and selections from the classics, chosen for their melodic beauty and technical value. They have been skillfully transcribed and edited by Samuel Applebaum, one of America's foremost teachers.

CELLO

DVORAK Concerto in B Minor Op. 104 (2 CD Set)	MMO CD 3701
C.P.E. BACH Concerto in A Minor	MMO CD 3702
BOCCHERINI Concerto in Bb, BRUCH Kol Nidrei	MMO CD 3703
TEN PIECES FOR CELLO	MMO CD 3704
SCHUMANN Concerto in Am & Other Selections	MMO CD 3705
CLAUDE BOLLING Suite For Cello & Jazz Piano Trio	MMO CD 3706

OBOE

ALBINONI Concerti in Bb, Op. 7 No. 3, No. 6, Dm Op. 9 No. 2	MMO CD 3400
TELEMANN Conc. in Fm; HANDEL Conc. in Bb; VIVALDI Conc.in Dm	MMO CD 3401
MOZART Quartet in F K.370, STAMITZ Quartet in F Op. 8 No. 3	MMO CD 3402
BACH Brandenburg Concerto No. 2, Telemann Con. in Am	MMO CD 3403
CLASSIC SOLOS FOR OBOE Delia Montenegro, Soloist	MMO CD 3404
MASTERPIECES FOR WOODWIND QUINTET	MMO CD 3405
WOODWIND QUINTETS minus OBOE	MMO CD 3406

GUITAR

BOCCHERINI Quintet No. 4 in D "Fandango"	MMO CD 3601
GIULIANI Quintet in A Op. 65	MMO CD 3602
CLASSICAL GUITAR DUETS	MMO CD 3603
RENAISSANCE & BAROQUE GUITAR DUETS	MMO CD 3604
CLASSICAL & ROMANTIC GUITAR DUETS	MMO CD 3605
GUITAR AND FLUTE DUETS Volume 1	MMO CD 3606
GUITAR AND FLUTE DUETS Volume 2	MMO CD 3607
BLUEGRASS GUITAR CLASSIC PIECES minus you	MMO CD 3608
GEORGE BARNES GUITAR METHOD Lessons from a Master	MMO CD 3609
HOW TO PLAY FOLK GUITAR 2 CD Set	MMO CD 3610
FAVORITE FOLKS SONGS FOR GUITAR	MMO CD 3611
FOR GUITARS ONLY! Jimmy Raney Small Band Arrangements	MMO CD 3612
TEN DUETS FOR TWO GUITARS Geo. Barnes/Carl Kress	MMO CD 3613
PLAY THE BLUES GUITAR A Dick Weissman Method	MMO CD 3614
ORCHESTRAL GEMS FOR CLASSICAL GUITAR	MMO CD 3615

BANJO

FLUTE

RECORDER

FRENCH HORN

TRUMPET

TROMBONE

DOUBLE BASS

TENOR SAX

ALTO SAXOPHONE

DRUMS

VOCAL

BASSOON

VIOLA

MUSIC MINUS ONE 50 Executive Boulevard • Elmsford New York 10523-1325